SUMMARY OF MEASURE WHAT MATTERS:

How Google, Bono, and the Gates Foundation Rock the World with OKRs

By

John Doerr
BlinkRead

BlinkRead

Copyright(c) 2020

Table of Content

SYNOPSIS:

Measure What Matters (2018) chronicles John Doerr's lifelong journey of helping organizations implement objectives and key results – otherwise known as OKRs. With the help of OKRs, companies like Google and nonprofits like the Gates Foundation have been able to transform the way they set goals to reach new heights.

ABOUT AUTHOR:

John Doerr is an American investor and venture capitalist who has mentored countless CEOs and founders on the magic of OKRs. In addition to working at venture-capital firm Kleiner Perkins, he served as a member of President Obama's Economic Recovery Advisory Board.

DISCLAIMER:

This book is a SUMMARY. It is meant to be a companion, not a replacement, to the original book. Please note that this summary is not authorized, licensed, approved, or endorsed by the author or publisher of the main book. The author of this summary is wholly responsible for the content of this summary and is not associated with the original author or publisher of the main book.

WHAT'S IN IT FOR ME? DISCOVER THE REVOLUTIONARY POWER OF OBJECTIVES AND KEY RESULTS (OKRS).

Have you ever worked for an organization that, if not entirely lacking a sense of direction, at least didn't seem like it knew where it was going? If so, you certainly aren't alone. Companies often have so many goals that they might as well have none at all, and workers are tugged in so many directions that they often feel utterly directionless.

So what's the solution to this sorry state of affairs? The answer is objectives and key results, or OKRs for short. By having a handful of flexible, reachable and transparent goals, organizations can work together in an efficient way to achieve success.

And OKRs don't only allow companies to continuously update, track and rewrite their goals. They also encourage a growth-centered philosophy that is bound to help companies of all sizes rethink their management strategy, thus increasing their potential for greatness.

In these blinks, you'll discover

how the author's attempt to win his girlfriend back led him to OKRs;

why Google uses three colors to track their goals; and

what iconic product stemmed from project Caribou at Google.

OKRS WERE BORN AT MICROCHIP GIANT INTEL, WHERE THE AUTHOR WORKED IN THE 1970S.

The plots of many classic stories and fairy tales hinge on the pursuit of love. But who would've thought that love would play a central role in a somewhat less fanciful tale – that of the author discovering business objectives and key results, or OKRs for short?

In the summer of 1975, author John Doerr was trying to win back his ex-girlfriend Ann. He knew she had a job in Silicon Valley, but he wasn't sure where. As fate would have it, however, he found her working at Intel, the company where he'd just scored an internship.

The love story ended happily in the end, with him and Ann getting back together (they're still married). And as their romance reignited, another inspiring story began: the author's discovery of OKRs.

The luminary behind OKRs was Andy Grove, one of Intel's cofounders. Then the vice president, he'd go on to become the CEO, and his visionary leadership would be integral to the company's transformation from a small business into the global giant it is today. The use of OKRs was, of course, a central part of his approach.

After getting hired, the author attended one of Grove's seminars, where he explained that OKRs aren't about what you know, but what you do with what you know. If you want things to get done, execution must trump knowledge.

For example, one of Intel's objectives (Os) at the time was to be number one in the midrange computer component industry. By setting just a few such objectives, Grove explained, the company as a whole could truly focus on pursuing them..

But how would they know that they'd reached this objective? That's where key results (KRs) come in, Grove went on. For example, one KR at the time was to "win" ten designs for the Intel 8085 microprocessor – a win being every time the microprocessor was used in products designed by other companies.

Such KRs had to be measured simply with a clear yes or no. Everyone involved – known as contributors – would have to be able to understand whether the KR had been met or not, without argument.

By implementing this management system at Intel, Grove was able to grow the company by 40 percent every year throughout his eleven-year tenure as CEO.

Seeing the impact of OKRs in action, the author began a lifetime of commitment to spreading this revolutionary management philosophy to other companies.

OKRs allow organizations to stay focused on reaching their goals.

Anyone who's worked at a high-performance organization is aware that to move ahead as a team, everyone needs to know which direction they're headed in. But what's equally important is knowing where one is not headed.

This brings us to the first of three important characteristics of OKRs: there should only be a handful of organization-wide OKRs at any one time. That way, everyone from top management to lower-level employees can stay focused on achieving a limited number of important goals – together.

Next, once management has determined these top-level objectives, between three and five KRs are needed per objective to help everyone at the company know when each objective has been reached. Any more than this, and focus will become diluted to the point where progress is hard to measure.

Finally, you'll need a clear time frame, so that departments across the organization can stay focused on collectively meeting deadlines. The author recommends setting OKRs every quarter to keep abreast of today's fast-paced market changes.

Every three months, then, your company should come together and see whether OKRs have been achieved, and whether or not you need to build upon existing progress – or set a new course.

Brett Kopf, CEO of Remind, employed OKRs at the recommendation of the author to transform his small education start-up into a company with millions of users.

After Remind hit the big time in 2014, with 300,000 downloads per day, Kopf realized his team of 14 needed to focus if they wanted to continue company growth.

Luckily, the author's venture-capital firm had provided Remind with Series B funding. It was during this time that he briefed Kopf on OKRs, which helped considerably when Remind faced the major test of figuring out how to most effectively allot time and energy across their rapidly growing organization.

For example, one of their most-requested features was to add a "repeated message" function, so that teachers wouldn't have to manually send out the same messages to students every week. But Remind's objective during that quarter was to increase teacher engagement, and since this "repeat" feature wouldn't have helped them meet this time-sensitive objective, it was shelved.

By using OKRs to stay focused on their objectives – and not get distracted – the company continued to grow, securing Series C funding of 40 million dollars and, by 2016, employing 60 people.

HAVING A TRANSPARENT, ALIGNED OKR SYSTEM HELPS ORGANIZATIONS MOVE FORWARD EFFICIENTLY – AND COLLABORATIVELY.

It's common sense that openness and honesty are key to any successful human relationship. So why should things be any different in your organization?

One important aspect of OKRs is that they must be transparent to everyone in your organization.

Research shows that being transparent with goals increases motivation. In a survey of 1,000 Americans, respondents indicated that they would be far more motivated to reach their goals if their fellow workers could view their progress.

OKRs are more than just the overarching business goals of an organization; teams, departments and individual employees use them for their own individual work as well. But once top-level and individual OKRs become part of an organization's public domain, they must be aligned to truly succeed. This means that employees' individual OKRs must align with the company's vision, as set out in the top-level OKRs.

However, this doesn't mean that employees' day-to-day work is dictated by those at the top. Such a top-down approach hinders autonomy in the workplace and decreases employee motivation. It's best to instate a hybrid approach that is both top-down and bottom-up; this will foster collaboration, transparency and innovation.

One way of doing this is the 20 percent time concept employed by Google. This allows engineers to spend one day's worth of time every week (20 percent of their workweek) on projects that they feel would contribute to Google's overarching top-level OKRs.

A result of this philosophy? A young Google engineer spent his 20 percent on a project called "Caribou" in 2001. Today, this project is known as Gmail, and it's the most popular email client in the world.

But alignment isn't always easy to implement.

Take Mike and Albert Lee's MyFitnessPal app. In 2013, the author explained the importance of OKRs for their company's continued growth.

As the Lee brothers implemented the system, they discovered that a great number of people had OKRs that weren't aligned with the company's overarching goals. Making matters worse, the lack of alignment between individual departments' OKRs meant that different teams were having problems reaching their individual OKRs. In short, coordination of OKRs was severely lacking.

So the Lee brothers scheduled a quarterly meeting with departmental heads. Each one presented their OKRs to the room and identified potential teams without whose collaboration their OKRs wouldn't succeed.

By doing so, they could dive into the quarter knowing that their teams wouldn't become overstretched, and would be able to depend on other teams for support.

BY CONSTANTLY TRACKING OKRS, ORGANIZATIONS CAN MAKE SURE THAT THEY'RE HEADING IN THE RIGHT DIRECTION.

You probably know that writing down a goal raises the chances of your reaching it. The same can be said for tracking your goals as you pursue them.

In fact, a California study showed that friends who both wrote down their goals and shared their progress with friends on a weekly basis were 43 percent more likely to achieve their objectives.

The same goes for organizational OKRs.

Google, for example, usually has monthly sit-downs where employees touch base on how they are getting along with their quarterly OKRs. Not only is progress discussed;

roadblocks are also pointed out and key results updated accordingly.

During such meetings – or, indeed, at any time in the quarterly OKR life cycle – four options are available to OKR contributors: continue, update, start and stop.

If an objective is on track, it makes sense to continue it. However, if external conditions have made key results unobtainable, then it's best to update them to meet new realities.

It might even be necessary to start a new OKR in the middle of the quarter. And, sadly, unsuccessful OKRs sometimes need to be put to rest, which means stopping it mid-cycle.

Remind's Brett Kopf once had to put a stop to an OKR that was meant to prototype a peer-to-peer payment system. Mid-cycle, he identified it as a failure, since it wasn't solving any clear problem, and so he canceled the objective immediately.

To replace it, he set a new OKR in motion — building a feature that allowed teachers to ask students whether they would participate in school events. It was an instant success.

How, though, can an OKR contributor best recognize how far along they've come in reaching their key results?

Google uses a 0-1.0 color-coded scale that enables OKR contributors to assess how successfully they've completed key results. 0.0 to 0.3 (red) means no progress has been made. 0.4 to 0.6 (yellow) means progress has been made, but key results remain unmet. And finally, 0.7-1.0 (green) is a sign of the key result having been successfully attained.

Intel used a similar scoring system. When the company wanted to demonstrate that its 8086 chipset had the best performance of any microprocessor in 1980, one of the key results was to send out 500 samples of its arithmetic coprocessor by the end of the quarter.

They managed to ship 470, which resulted in a KR score of 0.9. That's pretty successful!.

IMPLEMENTING STRETCH GOALS ALLOWS ORGANIZATIONS TO TRULY EXCEL.

In 1969, humanity set foot on the moon for the first time. This was a previously unimaginable, daunting feat with a high risk of failure, and it stretched NASA to its limits.

But once an organization has the necessary focus, alignment and tracking systems in place, such high-risk challenges can be undertaken. These challenges are called stretch goals.

Put simply, stretch goals are OKRs that are a daunting challenge to OKR contributors. Research backs up the effectiveness of stretch goals, with studies showing that stretched employees exhibit higher levels of motivation, productivity and engagement.

But how does an organization know whether stretch goals are right for them?

Well, at Google, OKRs are separated into two distinct categories: stretch objectives and committed objectives.

Whereas committed objectives usually have to do with day-to-day metrics such as sales or hiring, stretch objectives are all about bigger-picture ideas. And while committed objectives are meant to be met with 100-percent success, stretch objectives at Google fail about 40 percent of the time.

Now, unlike Google, not all companies have a safety net of cash to fall back on if a high-risk stretch OKR fails. But with enough cash on hand, stretch goals have the chance of a big payoff.

Take Google's web browser Chrome, for example. The initial 2008 OKR behind the development of the browser stated that the goal was to make browsing the web as quick and effortless as flipping through a magazine.

The Chrome team's first stretch goal was overambitious: they wanted to get 20 million weekly users by the end of 2008. But the difficulty of achieving this goal inspired the team to keep upping their development game and focusing on the end goal, however unreachable it seemed.

The goal of twenty million weekly users was only reached in early 2009, but that didn't deter the Chrome team from setting more stretch goals to keep up the challenge. For 2009, the stretch goal was set at 50 million, but they only reached 38. However, by 2010, they finally managed to meet their stretch goal of 111 million users.

Now, in 2018, Chrome is used by over a billion people on mobile devices alone!.

COUPLING OKRS WITH CONTINUOUS PERFORMANCE MANAGEMENT WILL HELP BRING ABOUT A TRANSPARENT, HEALTHY WORKPLACE CULTURE.

If you work for a large organization, it's possible that you've sat through an annual performance review. These reviews end up costing an average of 7.5 management hours per employee – a huge amount. Meanwhile, only six percent of HR leaders think the process is worth the cost.

Now, just imagine you're a manager with 30 employees under you. That would mean one and a half months of reviews!

Luckily, change is in the air. Not only have over fifty Fortune 500 companies gotten rid of annual performance reviews, but many are replacing them with continuous performance management and their associated instrument of change – CFRs.

CFRs are the OKRs of the HR world, and are all about having conversations with employees that entail both feedback and recognition.

CFRs are a two-way street. Instead of the unidirectional annual performance review, CFRs involve conversations where real-time feedback and recognition go both ways.

And, in the same way that OKRs replace annual goals, CFRs should happen regularly so that performance improvements can be made throughout the year.

As opposed to traditional annual reviews, which only answer whether or not employees have reached their annual goals, CFRs allow leaders and contributors to sit down and discuss vital topics. Is the objective you're working toward realistic? Is it even the right objective to be working on? And is it motivating?

Take Adobe, for example. It used to be that every February, right after the annual performance reviews, there would be a brief increase in voluntary attrition – that is, employee resignations and retirements.

However, after ditching their review system in favor of a CFR-esque system called "check-ins," Adobe's voluntary attrition has decreased dramatically.

It should be obvious at this point that implementing OKRs and CFRs at an organization will undoubtedly contribute to a better workplace culture. Having teams of contributors working toward common goals – coupled with transparent communication and individual accountability – should be a clear way to increase an organization's performance.

And whereas OKRs give meaning to contributors' goals, CFRs provide the life juice needed to complete them. Together with ambitious stretch thinking, organizations can use these techniques to reach for the stars, and nourish the optimistic and people-oriented workplace culture that comes with them.

After all, organizations that treat their employees as partners, not subordinates, tend to be the most successful.

FINAL SUMMARY.

The key message in these blinks:

When life spins out of control and relationships feel unmanageable, it's often because there's a lack of boundaries. Boundaries empower us to own and address our own problems, desires, and feelings. They help us support others in their problems without shouldering their burdens, and enable us to ask for and accept help. Boundaries aren't just necessary; they can be a source of love and joy in our lives.

Actionable advice:

Form a boundary support group.

It takes a lot of strength to identify, create, and maintain boundaries in your life. Ever heard the saying "strength in numbers?"

Form a boundary support group, where you can flex those boundary-setting muscles in safety. Discuss boundary-related successes and failures, and even test boundary-setting out on each other.

BLINKREAD

BlinkRead is dedicated to creating high-quality summaries of non-fiction books to help you through the bestseller list each week

We cover books in self-help, business, personal development, science & technology, health & fitness, history, and memoir/biography. Our books are expertly written and professionally edited to provide top-notch content. We're here to help you decide which books to invest your time and money reading.

Absorb everything you need to know in 20 minutes or less!

We release new summaries each and every week, so join our mailing list to stay up-to-date and get free summaries right in your inbox!

CPSIA information can be obtained
at www.ICGtesting.com
Printed in the USA
BVHW082139070521
606760BV00009B/2462